FILMPODIUM
IM 'STUDIO 4'
JAN.–MÄRZ
1996

JOHN FORD

(Sojourns is published by the Peaks, Plateaus & Canyons Association, a consortium of nonprofit educational organizations of like mission that supports research and education on the vast public lands on the Colorado Plateau. These cooperating associations, as they are known, earn their income by operating retail bookstores in national parks and forests, and on public lands managed by the National Park Service, USDA Forest Service, Bureau of Land Management, Fish and Wildlife Service, Bureau of Reclamation, and other land management agencies. Net proceeds from book sales and other enterprises are returned to the respective agencies to support further research and education. Collectively, the members of Peaks, Plateaus & Canyons Association (PPCA) operate 96 bookstores, six field institutes, and have contributed over $50 million toward mission goals in the past five years alone. When you visit the public lands of the Colorado Plateau, look for bookstores operated by PPCA partner organizations. Your purchase of educational materials in these stores directly supports the parks and public lands you are visiting.

THE PEAKS, PLATEAUS & CANYONS ASSOCIATION

Arizona Natural History Association
P.O. Box 20429
Sedona, AZ 86341 / (928)821-6277
www.AZNaturalHistory.org SOJO

Dixie/Arizona Strip Interpretive Association
345 East Riverside Drive
St. George, UT 84790 / (435) 688-3275
www.az.blm.gov/asfo/ASIA.htm § SOJO

Bryce Canyon Natural History Association
P.O. Box 640051
Bryce, UT 84764 / (435) 834-4781
www.brycecanyon.org § SOJO

Canyonlands Natural History Association
3015 S. Highway 191
Moab, UT 84532 / (435) 259-6003
www.cnha.org § SOJO

Capitol Reef Natural History Association
HC 70, Box 15
Torrey, UT 84775 / (435) 425-3791 x115
www.capitolreefnha.org §

Glen Canyon Natural History Association
P.O. Box 1835
Page, AZ 86040 / (928) 608-6068
www.GlenCanyonNHA.org § SOJO

Grand Canyon Association
P.O. Box 399
Grand Canyon, AZ 86023 / (928) 638-2481
www.grandcanyon.org §

Intermountain Natural History Association
2430 South 9400 East
Jensen, UT 84035 / (435) 789-8807
www.inhaweb.com §

Mesa Verde Museum Association
P.O. Box 38
Mesa Verde National Park, CO 81330 /
(970) 529-4445
www.mesaverde.org § SOJO

Petrified Forest Museum Association
P.O. Box 2277
Petrified Forest, AZ 86028 /
(928) 524-6228 x239
www.cybertrails.com/~pfma §

Public Lands Interpretive Association
6501 Fourth St. NW, Suite I
Albuquerque, NM 87107 / (505) 345-9498
www.publiclands.org §

Western National Parks Association
12880 N. Vistoso Village Drive
Tucson, AZ 85755 / (520) 622-1999
www.wnpa.org §

Zion Natural History Association
Zion National Park
Springdale, UT 84767 / (435) 772-3265 or 3264
www.zionpark.org § SOJO

School for Advanced Research on the Human Experience, SOJOURNS ASSOCIATE
P.O. Box 2188
Santa Fe, NM 87504 / (505) 752-7200
www.sarweb.org § SOJO

Cline Library, SPECIAL CONTRIBUTOR
Northern Arizona University
P.O. Box 60022
Flagstaff, AZ 86011 / (928) 523-5551
www.nau.edu/library

To receive a regular subscription to SOJOURNS, become a Sojourns-level member of any group listed above whose name is accompanied by SOJO.
Shop online where you see the § symbol.

EDITOR
PAM FRAZIER, Frazier Enterprises, Inc., Sedona, Arizona

ART DIRECTOR/DESIGNER & ASSOCIATE EDITOR:
CAROL HARALSON, Sedona, Arizona

CONTACT US:
carolharalson@esedona.net
pamfrazier605@msn.com
or at Peaks, Plateaus & Canyons Association
P.O. Box 20915, Sedona, AZ 86351
www.sojournsmagazine.org

EDITORIAL BOARD
PAULA BRANSTNER, National Park Service, retired
CHRIS EATON, Glen Canyon Natural History Association
PAM FRAZIER, Frazier Enterprises, Inc.
LYMAN HAFEN, Zion Natural History Association
CAROL HARALSON, Carol Haralson Books, Sedona, Arizona
RICHARD MILLETT, Intermountain Natural History Association
GAYLE POLLOCK, Bryce Canyon Natural History Association
SAM WAINER, Canyonlands Natural History Association

SOJOURNS welcomes comments and ideas for future themes and articles. Contributors are encouraged to visit the SOJOURNS page of the PPCA Web site for future themes and submission guidelines: www.sojournsmagazine.org. SOJOURNS is a benefit of membership at designated levels for members of most cooperating associations listed here. Individual copies are available in limited s at cooperating association bookstores across the Colorado Plateau. SOJOURNS published twice yearly. PPCA members proudly partner with the National Park Service, USDA Forest Service, Bureau of Land Management, U.S. Fish & Wildlife Service, and the U.S. Bureau of Reclamation.

Sojourns/At the Movies
Volume 8 Number 1 ~Winter/Spring 2013
©2013 by the Peaks, Plateaus & Canyons Association
All rights reserved | ISSN 1558-7738
Base map for Colorado Plateau map courtesy of U.S. Geological Survey, customized by Amanda Summers.
Printed in Korea by P. Chan & Edward

FRONT COVER: Farona Konopak stills and detail from film poster courtesy Rennard Strickland. Still from *3:10 to Yuma*, Photofest. Still from *Thelma and Louise*, Photofest. BACK COVER: *Stagecoach* poster, Photofest. PAGE ONE: Promotional poster for an international film symposium. Courtesy Rennard Strickland. PAGE THREE: Poster montage courtesy CNHA; background, Ema Dreamstime. CONTENTS PAGE: Top to bottom, strip by strip: The Lone Ran and Tonto, courtesy CNHA. Filming of *Stagecoach*, courtesy CNHA. Still from *Missing*, Hollywood stock photo courtesy Cathy Smith. The young Bette Stant courtesy Bette Stanton. Still from *Son of the Morning Star* mini-series. courtes Cathy Smith. Coral Pink Sand Dunes State Park, Utah, Kavram/Dreamstime. Farona Konopak, New Mexico State Records Center & Archives. A Harvey Girl at El Ortiz, Fred Harvey photo. Taos adobe, Benkrut/Dreamstime. Santa Fe sig Dreamstime. Sedona aerial by Ted Grussing.

WINTER/SPRING 2013

so journs

36

MOVING PICTURES
The Films of Farona Konopak

with **DOTTIE DIAMANT**

42+

Technicolor ROCKS
starring Sedona's own
JOE O'NEILL

Moab's Movie Museum
by **SAM WAINER**

meep meep!
and that's all, folks!

SANTA FE

JOHN A. MURRAY

FABLES AND DISTANCES

JUST AS EACH PERSON CREATES A PERSONAL HISTORY THAT IS PARTLY TRUE AND PARTLY MYTHIC, WEAVING FACT AND FICTION—WHAT HAPPENED, WHAT SORT OF HAPPENED, AND WHAT NEVER HAPPENED— SO DO A NATION'S FILMS.
IN THE FILMS OF THE SOUTHWEST—PARTICULARLY THOSE ANCHORED IN ACTUAL EVENTS—WE AS A NATION HAVE FABRICATED AN ALTERNATIVE AND OFTEN ILLUSORY VISION OF OURSELVES AND THE PAST.

I am sitting on a rock overlooking Monument Valley. It is the hour before sunrise. The sky to the west, over Oljeto Mesa, is still sprinkled with a few stars. The sky to the east, over the distant Chuska Mountains, is as pink as the palm of my hand. Even as I watch, a lens of red light is forming on the horizon. Before me are three great buttes—Left Mitten, Merrick, and Right Mitten. The names may not be familiar, but almost everyone has seen the formations, for they have been featured in dozens of films. For vast distances the landscape is perfectly flat, and then suddenly there are these three heavy solid rocks, each rising to the height of a one-hundred-story building. As the light comes up on the earth, the country begins to reveal its secrets. It is a desert land, spare and disciplined, and there is no fat on it. The colors are dry and sun-washed, like the colors of Anasazi pottery sherds. The floor of the desert is covered with reddish-brown sand, dotted here and there with rabbitbrush and sage, prickly pear cactus, and barbed yucca. Along the winding stream courses, junipers and pinyons grow, branched in delicate ways like bonsai. The early-morning air is cool and fresh, and scented with the smell of sage.

All narratives, all films, ultimately **are grounded in nature,** for nature consists of an endless series of stories.

All narratives, all films, are ultimately grounded in nature, for nature consists of an endless series of stories. We have, for example, the continual pageant of the seasons; the epic migrations of birds and beasts; the slow, steady passage of the days; the times of breeding and the times of birth; the building of great storms; the waxing and waning life and death of stars and galaxies; the life and death of the universe itself. Each of these would be stories even if there were no people around to tell them as stories. They exist, have existed, and will always exist, separate from the human experience. Creating a film—creating any narrative—is an act very much at one with the natural processes of the world.

All films, then, begin with a story. The direct sources of the narrative vary considerably. Sometimes, the inspiration for a film is a short story, as when John Ford used James Bellah's story "Massacre" for his 1947 film *Fort Apache*. The challenge that filmmakers face with short fiction is that, because of its abbreviated length, short fiction focuses primarily on one action or character. Neither is ordinarily sufficient to sustain a full-length movie. More commonly, the source of a film is a novel, as when Willa Cather's novel *Cheyenne Autumn* inspired the 1964 John Ford film of the same title, or when Vardis Fisher's novel *Mountain Man* stirred Robert Redford to produce his 1972 film *Jeremiah Johnson*. Novels have multiple characters, explore at least two characters in depth, and include a substantial series of organically linked scenes. More often than not, they also have a parallel or contrapuntal subplot. Occasionally a play serves as a source of a film, as when William Inge's Pulitzer-prize winning drama *Picnic* was transformed into the 1955 Oscar-winning movie of the same name. Plays, with their close attention to character, revelatory action, and dialogue, can serve quite naturally as the basis for films.

Most of the time, though, a film is based upon an original screenplay—a dramatic script that is written by professional screenwriters, often in cooperation with industry executives, specifically for the purpose of creating a particular movie. This has been true since the earliest days of silent film and was demonstrably the case during the "Golden Age of Film," when such writers as William Faulkner and F. Scott Fitzgerald were regularly called in to write or rewrite screenplays. This practice has continued into more recent times, as when Arthur Miller wrote the screenplay for John Huston's 1961 film *The Misfits* or Dalton Trumbo was hired to transform Edward Abbey's novel *The Brave Cowboy* into the 1962 film *Lonely Are the Brave*.

Screenplays (regardless of source) consist primarily of dialogue for characters, but may also contain detailed instructions regarding set location, camera placement, wardrobe, and even such matters as the sort of vocal tone, facile expression, and arm movements the actor should use. The screenplay provides the literal blueprint, or, to use another metaphor, the cellular DNA from which the film is made.

All successful movies, John Wayne once observed in a PBS interview toward the end of his career, are based on good characters. The key is what happens to the characters and how they react to the internal conflicts or external complications that develop as the story progresses. Sometimes a film focuses on a dialectic—on the relationship between two major characters. Other times, a film contains a buried triangle—three people whose interactions form the oldest structure in the geometry of drama. Much of the work in creating a screenplay focuses on building strong characters and then letting them interact naturally in ways the audience will find interesting or revealing.

Photofest

The **screenplay** provides the literal blueprint, or, to use another metaphor, the screenplay is **the cellular DNA from which the film is made.**

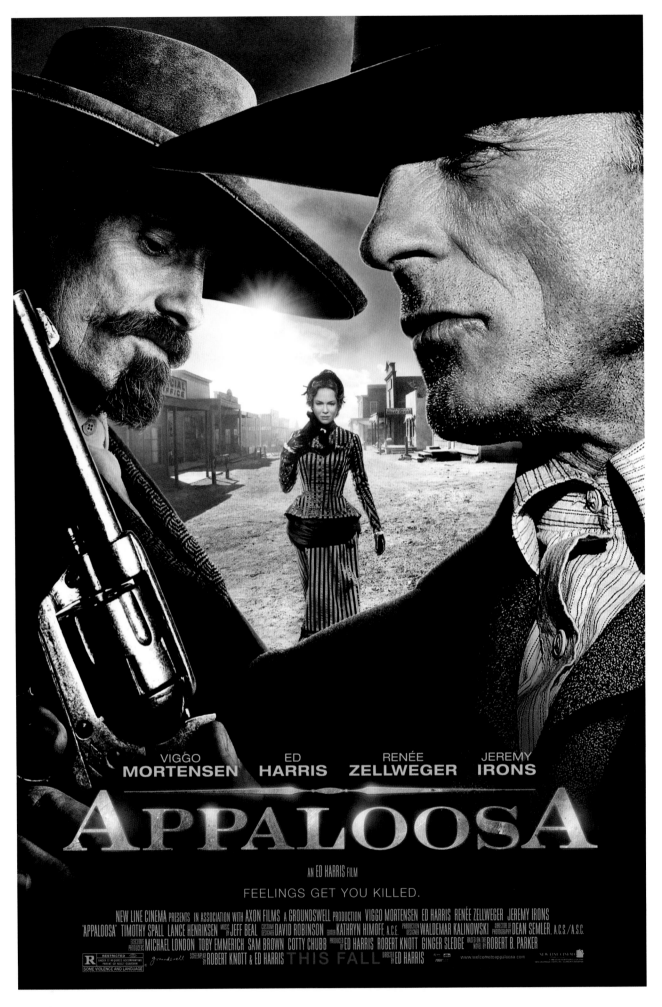

Photofest

After the screenplay has been more or less finalized, studio backing and financing must be arranged, the most difficult part of the filmmaking process. Many a worthy project has languished for years, or ultimately died, in this delicate embryonic phase. Making films is an expensive business compared to an artist painting a landscape or a writer composing a novel. Even in the 1930s, a major film production could cost as much as half a million dollars, as with John Ford's *Stagecoach*. By the 1990s, a minimal budget for a major motion picture budget was in the neighborhood of $20 million.

From top left: Paul Newman and Robert Redford in *Butch Cassidy and the Sundance Kid*. Photofest; Geena Davis and Susan Sarandon in *Thelma and Louise*. Photofest; Tom Mix and Zion area boys (l-r) Emil Justet, Victor Ruesch, Lloyd Crawford, and Lawrence Gifford, 1924.

The filming of *Stagecoach* in Monument Valley. Academy of Motion Pictures Arts and Sciences; Facing: Monument Valley. Fauro77photo/ Dreamstime

A film is, to paraphrase Thoreau . . . **at once more intimate and more universal** than any other work of art.

Once on location, a film can be compared to a traveling circus. It enters a town and everything in that community is immediately changed. Whatever was news the day before is forgotten. From that point forward, the town citizenry will measure the life of their town in terms of "before the movie" and "after the movie." Most noticeably, a film brings a rich infusion of cash directly into the community—lodging, meals, gas, assorted daily supplies for, sometimes, hundreds of employees. Also, local people must be hired to assist the filmmakers in myriad ways: drivers, carpenters, painters, plasterers, electricians, equipment handlers, laborers, technicians, wranglers, pilots, stunt doubles, set medics, cooks, production assistants, security guards, reclamation assistants, seamstresses, special experts (rock climbing, river rafting), and so forth. If shooting takes place on public land, then permits must be secured. Because films are such lucrative business, many towns (such as Moab, Utah, and Lone Pine, California) have for many decades had their own film commissions, which actively lobby studios.

One day, after many weeks, the filmmakers disappear. They return to their studios, which are usually in southern California, and then begin the sometimes tortuous process of editing the raw footage into a complete film. Test audiences watch the early edited versions, and their reactions are carefully analyzed. Were the characters well portrayed? Did the dialogue seem real? Was the musical score satisfying? Was the ending too happy or too sad? Would they recommend the film to a friend? Somehow in all this process an enduring work of art is created . . . or not. A date for release of the film is set. The actors, and sometimes the director, travel to the major movie markets and make advance appearances. We see them on Jay Leno or David Letterman talking about this or that aspect of filming. Articles are written. Critics weigh in based on their previews. Suspense gathers. Finally the film is released; it may be one of over three hundred films released that year. If the film is good, word spreads. If the film is bad, word spreads. Once in a while, the film is wonderful, a classic, a story for the ages and made so by instantaneous popular acclaim, and everyone is happy.

Just as each person creates a personal history that is partly true and partly mythic, weaving fact and fiction—what happened, what sort of happened, and what never happened—so do a nation's films provide their viewer with a series of narratives that soften the tragic, brighten the comic, and sharpen the historic. In the films of the

Southwest—particularly those anchored in actual events—we as a nation have fabricated an alternative and often illusory vision of ourselves and the past. Part of this is rooted in the very function of art. When Shakespeare wrote that "our little lives are rounded with a sleep" he expressed a statement the wisdom of which is not often fully appreciated. Films, like dreams or fables, are part of the protective membrane that memory and imagination generate over time, a metaphoric "sleep" that forms a boundary between each person, each society, and the cold, hard surface of history.

A film is, to paraphrase Thoreau's familiar passage on books, at once more intimate and more universal than any other work of art. It combines the ancient art of storytelling with the modern art of photography, the visual effects of landscape and portrait painting with the dramatic power of theater, the notes and chords of music with the rhythm and force of poetry. It is the work of art nearest to life itself. It may be viewed by people in any land, speaking any language, at any time, and not only be watched but, with the addition of subtitles or overdubbing, understood and enjoyed.

Movies are the treasured wealth of our time, and the highest creative expression of our age. They will be closely watched—for edification as well as entertainment—hundreds, thousands of years from now. Had Shakespeare been born in April of 1964 instead of April of 1564, he would now be active in films. He would be industriously writing and producing romances and comedies, histories and tragedies for the big screen, for film is to the Modern Age what verse drama was to the Elizabethan Age. Film is the most versatile tool ever given to the human imagination to explore the heights and the depths, the travail and the splendor, the mysteries and the paradoxes of the human experience.

OBSERVE THE PEOPLE EMERGING FROM A MOVIE THEATER. Study their faces. Each has been changed, if only for the evening, by the experience. Their tired faces are brightened or saddened, flushed with laughter or reddened with tears, furrowed in thought or blank with amazement, by what they have just witnessed. They carry with them the still-fresh images and impressions from that other world—the eternal world of art. Their generation will grow old and die. All they know will change and be changed again, but the film they have just watched will remain, the characters as timeless as the carved figures on Keats's Grecian urn, the drama enduring like an island against the relentless flow of time. Films, these viewers can attest, have power. They can change the world, if only one darkened theater at a time. Posterity will watch our films as the crowning artistic achievement of our age, as we now watch performances of Greek tragedy or Elizabethan drama. They will view these landscapes in the theater and want to return to view them in nature. It would be truly wonderful if they could still come out from the city and see the same undisturbed beauty that I view this morning.

JOHN A. MURRAY has taught at Regis University, the University of Denver, the University of Alaska, and elsewhere, and is the author of over forty works of nonfiction. This essay is excerpted from the expanded second edition of his *Cinema Southwest* (2011), published by Canyonlands Natural History Association. The book is available online at CNHA.org.

where god put the west

BETTE STANTON *with* CINDY HARDGRAVE

WHEN A TOURIST ASKED WHY THEY WERE FILMING IN MOAB,
ACTOR JOHN WAYNE RESPONDED, "TO FILM A REALLY BIG WESTERN,
YOU HAVE TO GO WHERE GOD PUT THE WEST. . . "

ollywood producers began leaving their studio sets to film amidst actual landscapes in the 1920s and '30s. They soon discovered the magnificent scenery of the Colorado Plateau—and the rest is movie history. Soon audiences around the world had come to recognize its rugged landscapes as being synonymous with "The West."

Monument Valley, located on the Arizona/Utah border, was the first to receive Hollywood. Harry Goulding, who lived on the Navajo Reservation during the Great Depression, traveled to Hollywood with a portfolio of landscape photographs to recruit filmmakers who could bring much needed jobs and money to the struggling population. Director John Ford liked what he saw and took his company there to film *Stagecoach* with John Wayne in 1939, where most of the stars and crew stayed at Goulding's Lodge. Ford returned many times.

By the 1940s Kanab, Utah, a little farther west, had become known as Little Hollywood. The varied scenery made Kanab a prime base for movie making. Located within an hour or so of Zion, Bryce Canyon, and Grand Canyon National Parks, it also had sand dunes nearby that were perfect for filming *Arabian Nights* (1942).

Ford eventually discovered Moab, Utah, located near today's Arches and Canyonlands National Parks, Castle and Professor Valleys, and Dead Horse Point State Park. His first film shot in Moab was *Wagon Master* (1949), the story of Mormon settlers moving west. By this time the importance of the movie industry in this area prompted the founding of the Moab to Monument Valley Film Commission, which is recognized as the longest running film commission in North America. At least fifty movies have been made in the Moab to Monument Valley area since then.

HARDGRAVE: How did you get involved in the movie industry, Bette?

STANTON: All the makings for western movies can be found in my family history. My paternal great-grandfather was one of the first settlers in the Moab area. He was a Mormon polygamist who emigrated from Denmark to the "Promised Land." He had encounters with Indians, as well as Butch Cassidy and the Wild Bunch. Range wars were part of life then, too. He had confrontations with bears, rattlers, and cougars; the family lived on sego lily bulbs and pigweed for an entire winter. Of course, I came along much later. In 1938, my parents moved our family to Kanab, and by that time Kanab was already becoming well known as one of the few locations where movies were filmed away from the big studios in Hollywood. Kanab was a small town with a population of about 800. Most people's livelihoods revolved around livestock. This was still the Wild West. There were no tourists and that's why they were romancing the film industry so much, because it was bringing work and spreading money throughout the town. By the 1940s, *Life* magazine had done a special article on Kanab, dubbed it "Little Hollywood," and that's what put Kanab on the map for tourists. That gave us an additional income.

H: What movies were you in and what jobs did you perform?

S: I was about twelve when I started getting involved with movies. I think the first one was *Green Grass of Wyoming* (1948). Part of it was filmed at Three Lakes, which is a popular location about eight miles up the canyon from Kanab. They have a big dance hall that goes out over the lake; they used that a lot in some of the movies. After that I worked on *Red Canyon* (1949). That one was shot during school, and the kids and our teachers were all in it. Then came *The Outriders* (1950), with Joel McCrea and Arlene Dahl. They needed somebody with long, blonde hair to stand in for Arlene Dahl. I was only fourteen and you couldn't get hired to double or stand in unless you were eighteen. But Arlene Dahl had major surgery, so I wound up having to take everything but lines and close-ups.

H: That must have been quite an experience for a teenager.

Bette Stanton (she was Bette Larsen then) when she was a stand-in for Arlene Dahl in *The Outriders.* Courtesy of Bette Stanton; Facing: Hasenonkel/ Dreamstime

Director John Ford and John Wayne on the set of *Horse Soldiers* (1959). Photofest Facing: Monument Valley. Chrismr/Dreamstime

S: People think Hollywood is glamorous but it's not, because you work some of the longest hours in the world. Before you even start work on set, you have to get up in time for makeup and wardrobe. And dressing up wasn't always fun. They cinched me into a corset that gave me a nineteen-inch waistline, which overlapped my ribs, and every time I laughed or coughed it was like being electrocuted. And I had a sixteen-pound petticoat to pack around all day! You travel miles to get to location, film until sundown, get back after dark to check in all of your stuff, and you're lucky if you get home in time to get any sleep. Then you get up and do it again the next day.

That reminds me of *Westward, the Women* (1951), with Robert Taylor and Denise Darcel. I got a pretty good break on that one. Robert Taylor played a wagon master bringing all these women from the East to be wives of the men in the West. This time we had to wear army boots, and there was one scene at Paria (east of Kanab) where we supposedly hadn't seen water for a hundred miles; when we saw it, we all had to run into it. We'd jump down from the wagons and start running for the water—the mules, the horses, the women, everything. We had to wade clear into the water and splash through it. Then they'd yell, "Cut! Take it again!" and we had to climb out with wet army boots and wet clothes and trot clear back to the wagons and start all over again. By the time we got to the wagons we were pretty well dry because it was a ways to go, jumping over sagebrush and all.

H: Tell us about some of your memorable moments with stars and directors.

S: As far as the directors go, Ford was great. He was real open and relaxed, wonderful. Nowadays, everybody's on edge. I really liked Burt Reynolds. He was so down to earth. I even dated him for a while. Those were the good old days. I am so blessed to have been here through all that.

Director John Ford and actor Tim Holt on the set of *Stagecoach* (1939), in Monument Valley. Photofest

H: What were some of the challenges of working on location on the Colorado Plateau?

S: Well, these folks from Hollywood aren't always up on our desert climate. A lot of people don't realize how hot and dry we get here. In the old days, they had tents and things for people to get under. When they yelled, "Cut! Rest until the clouds get back," you went into the shaded areas that they kept for you. The stars had their special chairs and they had water right at their fingertips. But more recently we did a science fiction movie here and everyone was dressed in really heavy costumes. The temperature got up to 117° F., and we had people dropping from heat exhaustion because they weren't taken care of properly.

John Ford had an Indian medicine man on set. As the story goes, this medicine man could predict the weather and Ford had him at his elbow at all times so he could work his script and his planning right into what took place. One thing about John Ford: he often played into whatever was happening. Sometimes the weather itself became a character and it made the movie much better.

Then you had the challenges of the companies coming out to the wilderness. They brought lots of big camera and sound equipment and they need to bring crews to the sites in big buses. And we didn't even have paved roads through Moab back then. We didn't have all the conveniences you do with the big sets in Hollywood. Worst of all, we didn't have accommodations. We were not a tourist town then—we were a mining town and cattle town.

H: So how did they accommodate them?

S: They put up tents for the crew and the stars went into local homes—that's how we had to take care of them. And we had only a couple of restaurants then, too. Probably the accommodations and the geography were toughest on them. Now, of course, we're better equipped.

H: How did shooting in wilderness affect the land?

S: That's a very good question. The movie makers took care of the land because they wanted it to be pristine. They were filming Westerns in the days before utilities went in; everything was gorgeous and fresh, and nothing was more important to them than preserving it.

Of course, that's not always the case today. This is where film commissions come into play. They keep peace between the film crews and the locals. What our commission did, after a movie was here, was to have town hall meetings where people could talk about anything that had gone wrong, so we wouldn't repeat it the next time around. We got everyone together— the permit people from the Bureau of Land Management, national parks, state parks, the mayor, the chairman of the county commission, the state director of the film commission—so that the audience could express any frustrations: whether they didn't get paid or whether the place was torn apart. We would record this and report it to the Association of Film Commissioners International.

H: Is shooting commercials any different from shooting movies?

S: We do better squeezing in crews for commercials than for feature films. Movies like to film in the summer because of the long hours of sunlight. Well, that's our most popular tourist season, and everything in town is full—no room for the movies. Shooting commercials is short-term and the crews are smaller. You cannot turn on your television today and not see our country in commercials—even cartoons.

H: Would you say that the film industry marketed Colorado Plateau geology? They made this country sing to the hearts of millions of people around the world.

S: Do you know how many foreign people we get here who say, "I feel like I'm coming home!"? Yes, the film industry markets this land—gives people awareness of its beauty; creates an emotional connection. The star of all these movies, of all these commercials, of all these television shows is the scenery, the country! That's what inpires us all.

Marilyn Monroe and Don Murray in the Joshua Logan–directed Western *Bus Stop* (1956). Photofest

dressing the west

with costume designer **CATHY SMITH**

"TO TRANSFORM ONE HUNDRED MOVIE EXTRAS INTO WARRIORS WEARING BUCKSKIN AND MOCCASINS, WAR PAINT AND FEATHERS, AND THEN TO SEE THEM ON HORSEBACK SILHOUETTED AGAINST THE HORIZON OF AN EPIC LANDSCAPE—THAT IS THE MAGIC THAT KEEPS ME IN THE BUSINESS OF MOTION PICTURE COSTUME DESIGN."

Costume in the movies is about storytelling, about bringing a director's vision to life. Great costumes are so much more than mere fashion; they reflect and augment the development of a character: her emotional journey, status, personality, and the cultural and temporal landscape that surrounds and affects her. Many cultural touchstones have been created by costume designers, from the starched uniforms in Edwardian "upstairs/downstairs" dramas to the turned-up collars of disaffected teens in 1950s hot rod movies to the ball gowns worn by Jane Austen heroines. But designers are by definition invisible. A great costume should never look like a "costume." It should be so authentic to time, place, character, and story that it feels natural and "undesigned."

My specialty is western and Native American costume. This interest did not originate in Hollywood, but on a ranch on the Cheyenne River Sioux Reservation where I was raised surrounded by cowboys and Indians—the real thing! The Saturday matinee Westerns at our local theater were the exciting event of the week. We each took our twenty-five cent piece and bag of penny licorice into the darkened theater with great anticipation. But for me these movies were often an embarrassment: John Wayne fought white men dressed as Indians; Tonto, and even *A Man Called Horse,* looked ridiculous in faux leather. This was the Myth of the West in Technicolor, a popular image of a frontier that never was. A majority of these films were shot in the valleys and canyons of the Colorado Plateau, locations of epic grandeur, but not actually the habitat of the Plains Indians they featured. Nor were the costumes in most of these movies historically accurate.

The Searchers, filmed in Monument Valley in 1956, is considered by many to be a true American masterpiece of filmmaking and perhaps the most admired film of director John Ford. But the story takes place in Texas, which doesn't look at all like Monument Valley, and John Wayne's character, an affirmed Rebel, wears Union cavalry trousers with his Confederate cape. Scar, the Comanche chief, is played by Henry Brandon, a blue-eyed Anglo in a braided wig and faux leather. Natalie Wood's character, Debbie, becomes the wife of Scar, but is dressed in Navajo velveteen, not Comanche buckskin.

Geronimo has been the subject of at least three major motion pictures filmed on or near the Colorado Plateau. The first, shot in 1939, starred Victor Daniels or Chief Thunder Cloud, a mixed-blood Cherokee actor. The tagline read: *The Red Raider roars into battle…with 10,000 yelling Indians at his back! Thrill to the heart-thudding courage of a boy and a girl who risked their very lives for their love…who dared the ruthless wrath of the war-mad demon, Geronimo!* Costumed much like Tonto in the famous Lone Ranger series, Geronimo wears what looks like a faux leather leisure suit and a thin buckskin headband, which serves to keep the wig in place.

Top: Natalie Wood in *The Searchers.* Hollywood stock photo.
Facing: Gary Sundown as Hiawatha in a documentary on the Iroquois. Photo by Jennifer Jesse Smith.

GERONIMO!

ctor Daniels played the first Geronimo in 1939
oove right), costumed much like Tonto in The
ne Ranger series. The second Geronimo was
ayed by Chuck Connor (above left) in 1962.
nnor wore tight-fitting blue cloth pants and
hort-sleeved V-neck pullover. In 1993 Walter
l directed the most recent version of the
ronimo story, *An American Legend*, starring
manche actor Wes Studi (right). It was shot in
onument Valley. Cathy Smith created Studi's
stume based on research that included the
tual Geronimo's original cap, now in the
uthwest Museum in Los Angeles. Photos
ove and right courtesy Cathy Smith.

A Scene from *Comanche Moon*, Larry McMurtry's prequel to *Lonesome Dove*, shot in New Mexico. Photo courtesy Cathy Smith

Cultural markers are important to all people, **identifying the truth of their lives.**

The second version of Geronimo was played by Chuck Connor in 1962. Connor was in tight-fitting blue cloth pants and a short-sleeved, fringed, V-neck pullover cut to show his chest almost to the waist. His co-star, Kamal Devi, wears a short cotton dress that reveals her bare legs, something an Apache woman would never do.

Walter Hill directed the most recent version of the Geronimo story, *An American Legend* (1993), starring Comanche actor Wes Studi. It was shot in Monument Valley and around Moab, Utah, not exactly Apache land, but close. I was hired by designer Dan Moore to create historically accurate costumes for Geronimo and the main Apache characters in the film. Researching Geronimo, I found his original war cap and other personal items in the storage vaults of the Southwest Museum in Los Angeles and duplicated these items using the same materials and techniques used by the Apache in 1880. We matched Studi's look as closely as possible to the photos of Geronimo.

There is no lack of period photographs of Geronimo. Dozens of photos were taken and they have been published extensively. Unlike Chief Scar in *The Searchers*, Geronimo was not a fictional character, but a very famous war chief, even though on the big screen he has often been fictionalized, as has his clothing. As the last hostile chief to hold out against the United States government's policy of manifest destiny, he became known to households across America. But the Apache were very different in dress and appearance from the classic "Noble Savage" thought of by most Americans. Not nearly as romantic, they didn't wear buckskin and feathers and beads. Or live in tipis. The Apache lived in brush wickiups in the mountains of Arizona and Mexico, raiding in both directions. By the 1880s the men were wearing cotton peon pants and cotton breechcloths and the women wore wide-tiered cotton calico skirts. Buckskin moccasins that extended thigh-high, with rounded, curled up cactus-kicker toes prevailed against the rough terrain. The men wore wide cloth headbands to keep their long hair out of the way. The women's hair was chopped to shoulder length and unadorned. Cultural markers are important to all people, identifying the truth of their lives.

As well as being historically accurate, good costumes must say something about character and plot. Does the bad guy always wear a black hat? Does John Wayne's shirt fade in the sun, fray, and become worn and soiled after a long journey through the desert? Does Kevin Costner as Lieutenant Dunbar "go Injin" in *Dances with Wolves*? That was a big question for us working on *Dances*. Would his character change enough through his association with the Lakota to adopt native clothing? We decided it did. But not until the last moment. I had to make his buckskin shirt overnight and do the beadwork on Costner's shoulders while riding with him to the set. Mornings are always stressful for the costume crew, some more than others.

Dances with Wolves, shot in 1989, was among the first films to attempt to portray Native Americans in all their humanity and complexity. And I believe it was the first time Native costumes and sets were historically accurate. We were given ten weeks to create all of the costumes from scratch, including doubles and triples for the stars and the stunts. All of those porcupine-quilled buckskin warshirts were made in duplicate or triplicate, one for the actor, one the stunt double, and one for the photo double. If a scene calls for a battle, blood, or an arrow hit, five or six copies of each costume are made. They never get it in one take! A crew of six, we worked eighteen hours a day to handsew, bead, and quill the buckskin costumes. Then of course, they all had to be "aged," or given a patina, so they

As Kicking Bird in *Dances with Wolves*, Graham Green wears a historically accurate porcupine-quilled, human hair-trimmed warshirt, leggings, and bear claw necklace made by Smith. Photo courtesy Cathy Smith

looked worn and lived in. Using soil samples from the area, we concocted a mixture of fuller's earth and pigments, oils, and earth, to wear down the newly made costumes.

Research for *Dances with Wolves*, whose time period is circa 1860, involved studying the journals and illustrations left by early explorers to the West. Since this was pre-camera, there were no historic photos available. The journal of Prince Maximilian zu Weid, with the accompanying illustrations of Karl Bodmer, became the basis for our costumes, including color and design. And speaking of color, the designer must work within the color palette chosen by the production designer, so that the overall look of the film stays within a range of compatible hues.

Brain-tanned buckskin was the material of choice in the 1860s. To create it, deer hides are tanned with brains, resulting in a soft pure white hide, which was often smoked to give it a buckskin color and water resiliency. Our first job was to find more than 600 deer hides with the look of brain-tanned hide. We had other fabric custom-woven to get the correct period colors and weave.

As well as being historically accurate, good costumes must say something about character and plot. **Does the bad guy always wear a black hat?**

Once the costumes were finished, we started fittings with the actors that would result in changes to accommodate their personal needs, hopes, and fears. Clothing is a very personal thing: the material and fit must feel good on the body, it must be strong enough to withstand horseback stunts, often it must be fire-proofed, and it must augment the character. The shape of the silhouette is indicative of character as well as era. Period undergarments are often required to create the correct shape.

And the actor must feel comfortable, so that he can do his job. Sometimes this is a difficult goal to reach, especially if the scene says it's summer and the actor is wearing only a breechcloth and moccasins, but the outside temperature is really 30° F. We went through a lot of queen-size panty hose!

When the shooting starts, the real fun begins. Since a film is not shot in sequence, a continuity book is kept with photos and descriptions of each scene. We might shoot scene 25 this morning and scene 90 this afternoon, so someone has to keep track of how many feathers were in Kicking Bird's hair and at what angle, how dirty his shirt was, whether the neck button was open or not, so that when we do the following scenes weeks later, we get the continuity right. I'm sure you've all seen movies with little discrepancies in the continuity.

An accurately dressed Apache from *The Missing*, filmed in New Mexico. Hollywood stock photo courtesy Cathy Smith

Smith repairing a stunt man's costume on the set of *Dances with Wolves*. Photo courtesy Cathy Smith

A day in the life of filming *Dances With Wolves* began at 3:30 AM in the middle of a 65,000-acre buffalo pasture.

A day in the life of filming *Dances With Wolves* began at 3:30 AM on location in the middle of a 65,000-acre buffalo pasture fifty miles from town. Imagine the day every costumer dreads: the first time in the filming that we have to dress a large group of extras. How fast can we dress 150 Lakota men, women, and children whom we've never seen before? We had no pre-fittings, so could only hope we had enough clothing that fits. And it is not true that just because one is a registered member of the Lakota nation, he knows how to put on a breechcloth!

Dressing in tents in the pre-dawn twilight, we tie up leggings, hide bra straps, remove watches and modern jewelry, make instant blanket dresses for little girls, and get everyone through wardrobe and into the hair and makeup trailers. Then into buses, which transport us from base camp to the set, along with our tools, leather thongs, and needles and sinew for instant repairs.

By now it is around 10:00 AM. The 150 extras are bringing home the meat from the buffalo hunt. Little children and eighty-year-old grandmothers and grandfathers are among the warriors. Everything is going well until we discover that we're in a pasture teeming with prickly pear cactus that cut right through moccasin soles. Between each take, armed with pliers, we pull stickers out of feet.

1:00 PM: The extras are strung out for a quarter mile leading horses loaded with buffalo meat and parfleche. A herd of 300 horses follows the moving camp, the pony herd that is ever present in each camp scene. Some of the horses are rented from a local rodeo string of bucking horses, and when a sudden prairie thunderstorm came upon us—lightning flashing and thunder booming—those horses break and stampede. Running through the line of people, they spook the travois horses so much that they buck their loads and scatter. People are stumbling, running, and getting trampled, all the while being pelted with rain and hail. Of course there is not a tree or shelter in sight. The prairie turns to gumbo, slippery and sticky, building up on moccasin soles and sticking to buckskin.

We finally manage to get all the extras back to the buses and start drying them off. This was the first time we had used 150 buckskin costumes and now they are wet and muddy. Thankfully no one was hurt.

7:00 PM: We finally have everyone dried out and the horses caught so we can shoot the scene. Instead of an afternoon shot, we get a silhouette shot against the setting sun. At 10:00 PM we all travel back to base camp where the extras change clothes, leaving the costume crew to work all night scraping mud and horse manure off the bottoms of 300 moccasins. All must be ready for tomorrow's 3:00 AM call.

Other days are not as difficult. However, shooting a Western is always a challenge.

I'm often asked why something was done a certain way in a film and my answer is this: You have to understand the odds stacked against you. When you are choreographing wild animals, horses, buffalo, wolves, and "wild Indians" out in the prairie weather, anything can happen, and it's seldom in your control. In fact, it's a wonder that anything ever gets to print at all.

Costuming a Western is a demanding experience that totally absorbs the designer's life for many months. It requires diligent research, artistic inspiration, creative skill, physical endurance, and a love of the subject. For me, it is a time machine wherein I can go back and live for a time in the past. It is like seeing history. I've fought the Battle of Little Big Horn at least six times, ridden with Geronimo across Monument Valley, chased Lightning Jack through Antelope Canyon and Quanah Parker across the Llano Estacado, and followed Crazy Horse through the Badlands. The best part is that it is recorded on film forever, but that is why it is so important to get it right.

CATHY SMITH is known for her costumes in films such as *Dances with Wolves, Comanche Moon, Geronimo,* and *Son of the Morning Star* (for which she won the Emmy for Costume Design). She restores original artifacts and creates custom clothing and accoutrements for film, museums, and clients worldwide, lecturing and exhibiting at venues from the Smithsonian to the Eiteljorg and the National Cowgirl Museum. She has long participated in the cultural lifeways of relatives on the Cheyenne River Reservation. Currently she is painting the Plains Indians she loves and knows so well, trading buckskin and sinew for oil and canvas. www.cathyasmith.com.

Seventh Cavalry riding to the Little Big Horn in *Son of the Morning Star* mini-series. Photo courtesy Cathy Smith

HI-YO SILVER
THE LONE RANGER RIDES AGAIN

with
ROBERT LIVINGSTON
CHIEF THUNDER-CLOUD
SILVER CHIEF · DUNCAN RENALDO

Directed by WILLIAM WITNEY · JOHN ENGLISH
Associate Producer · ROBERT BECHE

A *Republic* SERIAL IN

15 *Whirlwind* CHAPTERS

Based on the Radio Serial, "THE LONE RANGER" by FRAN STRIKER

CHAPTER **12** **BLAZING PERIL**

just like in the movies

The Image of the Indian in Film

RENNARD STRICKLAND

DURING THE SHOOTING OF ONE OF JOHN FORD'S EPIC WESTERNS IN MONUMENT VALLEY,
THE CAMERAS STOP AND THE NAVAJOS DISMOUNT AND TAKE OFF THEIR SIOUX WAR BONNETS.
ONE OF THE CREW SAYS, "THAT WAS WONDERFUL, YOU DID IT JUST RIGHT."
AN INDIAN REPLIES, "YEAH, WE DID IT JUST LIKE WE SAW IN THE MOVIES."

Surely no racial, ethnic, or political group has been subjected to as much or as frequent on-screen stereotyping as have Native Americans. Film gave light and motion to long-standing images of deeply entrenched stereotypes. The Indian in film is rooted in more than 500 years of portrayals of Indians, in art and literature and commerce. Movies took the advertising posters off the barroom wall and flickered them through the nickelodeon. Budweiser's famous 19th-century advertising poster, "Custer's Last Fight" (1886), has been seen again and again as the climax to yet another screen version of the Battle of Little Bighorn. The screen Indian is, with few exceptions, directly out of the Indian captivity, travel, and exploration narratives, and such stalwart literary traditions as James Fenimore Cooper and the dime novel.

The transformation from Indian medicine show to Wild West Show, to nickelodeon, to two-reeler, to wide-screen epic was neither as long or as great as some fans of the cinema might suspect. Buffalo Bill, the Miller Brothers, and the

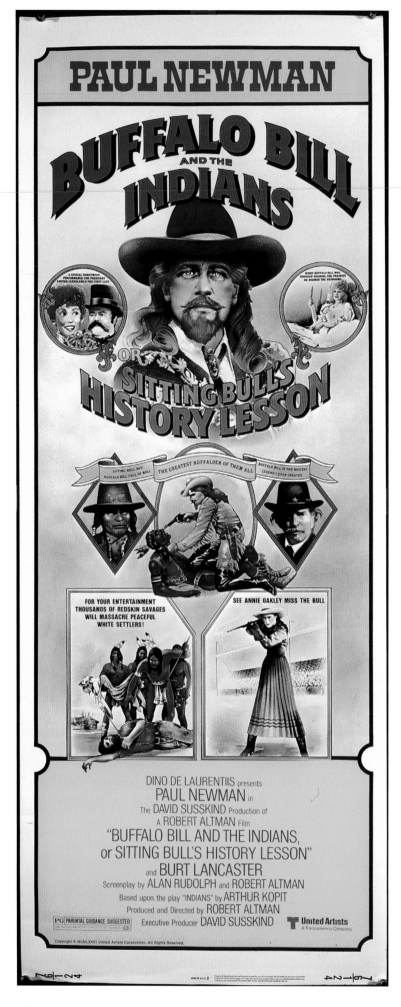

Photofest

101 Ranch Show were all involved in making movies in the early days of the silent screen. Many early Indian screen performers as well as film producers came directly from the whoop 'em up, wild and wooly tent-show tradition. As early as 1894 Buffalo Bill and his company paraded before Edison's Kinetoscope peep-show camera. And both sinister portrayals and historic distortions date from the very beginning. As early one- and two-reeler silents were replaced by ten- and twelve-reelers, longer and more sophisticated films portrayed Indian-white conflicts. The dividing line between the old-style William Ince and D. W. Griffith silents and the new silent western epics comes with James Cruz's *The Covered Wagon* (1923), followed quickly by John Ford's heroic *The Iron Horse.*

Little changed with the advent of sound. *The Big Trail* (1930), first of the western talkies, failed at the box office, sentencing its star, John Wayne, to wait in the wings for director John Ford to appear. In the 1930s Indians settled into the Saturday Kiddie Matinees, Poverty Row studio productions, Gene and Roy and Hopalong Cassidy adventures, with only an occasional big-budget remake of something like *The Last of the Mohicans* (1936).

It was not until 1939, when John Ford stunned the public with *Stagecoach,* that Indian films were once again a live genre. Between 1940 and 1950, big stars and big bucks were lavished on winning the West and fighting the Indians. *Broken Arrow* (1950) dramatically shifted the focus of the modern Western by creating Indians who were victims, not villains. It was a top grosser, setting the pattern for a new variation on Native stereotypes: nobility.

The popular image of the Indian in the post–World War II Western is primarily the creation of John Ford and John Wayne. These Westerns include his

Director John Ford on the *Cheyenne Autumn* set with Richard Widmark and Carroll Baker. Photofest

Posters reproduced in this essay and throughout the issue are in the Rennard Strickland Collection and shown courtesy of Rennard Strickland, unless otherwise noted.

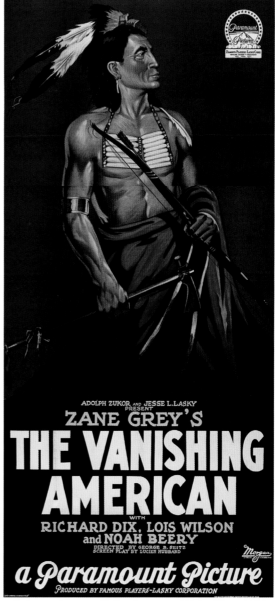

famous "cavalry trilogy," and the gentle, underrated *Wagonmaster* (1950), in which Indian-white conflict is peaceably resolved; *Cheyenne Autumn* (1964), which the director says was his effort to set the record straight, having killed off more Indians on screen than the entire Seventh Cavalry; and *The Searchers* (1956), a great compendium of all the images of the Indian, and a film with the ambiguity necessary to shatter those stereotypes.

In the late 1960s, change came to America and to Indian films. Jane Fonda's ex-husband Tom Hayden wrote a book, *The Love of Possesssions Is a Disease with Them* (1972), drawing the analogy between the massacres on the Northern Plains and the Southeast Asian jungles. In *Soldier Blue* (1970) and *Little Big Man* (1970), the film Indian became the reflection of white society's contemporary dilemmas.

John O'Connor, in his book *The Hollywood Indian* (1980) argues that the public issues of the day dominate Hollywood Indian movies. For example, Warner Brothers' *Massacre* (1934) is the product of the New Deal, with the Indian as the symbol of the struggles of Franklin Delano Roosevelt against corruption and the Great Depression. By 1939 and 1940, *Drums Along the Mohawk* and *They Died With Their Boots On* made the case that the world must be prepared to fight the Nazi savages to preserve civilization. The Indian as savior reemerged in the 1980s and 1990s, as new-agers and green revolutionaries espoused an ecological balance associated with the idealized Native lifestyle. Walt Disney released *Pocahantas* (1995) at the height of this frenzy.

Why should it matter to us how Indians have been presented in film? Because it transcends entertainment. It influences law. It affects resource management. The media profoundly impacts every aspect of contemporary American Indian policy and shapes both the general cultural view of the Indian as well as Indian self-image. The power of film can be seen from the smallest details

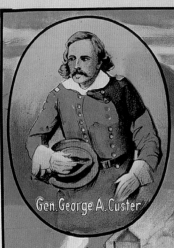

Gen. George A. Custer

Sitting Bull

Quality Amusement Corp.

PRESENTS

"Custer's Last Fight"

THE GREATEST WILD WEST FEATURE EVER FILMED

A Thomas H. Ince Special Production

OTIS
LITHOGRAPH CO

of an everyday children's game of cowboys and Indians to the international arena where a movie-star president of the United States gives Hollywood-rooted answers to Soviet students' questions about the Native Americans. As John Ford's newspaperman says at the end of *The Man Who Shot Liberty Valance* (1962), "This is the West. When the legend becomes fact, we print the legend." The legend is central to a beautiful short film called *Geronimo Jones* (1970), about a young Indian boy faced with a difficult decision. Should he trade an old Indian medal his grandfather has given him for a new television set? He agonizes over the question and finally decides. The

family gathers around the new electronic box and the first thing they see is the savage Indian of the classic Western. They see him again and again in the days that follow. Certainly this confusion of images affects the attitudes of Native groups toward themselves, but because of the way tribal resources are held in trust under U.S. government management and regulation, it affects their lives on many other levels.

A cinematic vision of the Indian includes: the Indian as bloodthirsty and lawless savage; the Indian as enemy of progress; the Indian as tragic but inevitable victim; the Indian as lazy, fat, shiftless drunk; the Indian as oil-

A cinematic vision of the Indian includes: bloodthirsty and lawless savage; enemy of progress; tragic but inevitable victim; lazy, fat, shiftless drunk; oil-rich illiterate; educated half-breed unable to live in either the white or the Indian world; nymphomaniac or bronze-armed Lothario; and the Indian as the first conservationist.

rich illiterate; the Indian as educated half-breed unable to live in either the white or the Indian world; the Indian as nymphomaniac or bronze-armed Lothario; the Indian as the first conservationist. Non-Indian filmmakers have been plumbing this well of stereotypical Indian images for well over a century now. Happily, Native American filmmakers, actors, critics, and producers now begin to tell their own stories, and a maturing filmgoer's consciousness accepts, even welcomes, new forms of narrative. Perhaps we may yet build a bridge from imagined past to authentic present.

RENNARD STRICKLAND is a legal historian of Osage and Cherokee heritage who is frequently cited by courts and scholars for his work as revision editor-in-chief of the *Handbook of Federal Indian Law.* He was founding director of the Center for the Study of American Indian Law and Policy at the University of Oklahoma and is the first person to have served both as president of the Association of American Law Schools and as chair of the Law School Admissions Council. Strickland is Distinguished Professor Emeritus and retired dean of the University of Oregon School of Law. This essay is based on "Tonto's Revenge, Or, Who Is That Seminole in the Sioux Warbonnet? The Cinematic Indian!" in *Tonto's Revenge: Reflections on American Indian Culture and Policy* (University of New Mexico Press, 1997), first presented as a lecture at the University of New Mexico.

Farona Konopak was born in Philadelphia in 1895, but her enduring love was the Southwest.

From her first visit in 1918, she embraced the landscape, the history, the culture, and the people.

She would in time record them on film, first for Fred Harvey and later in her own home movies.

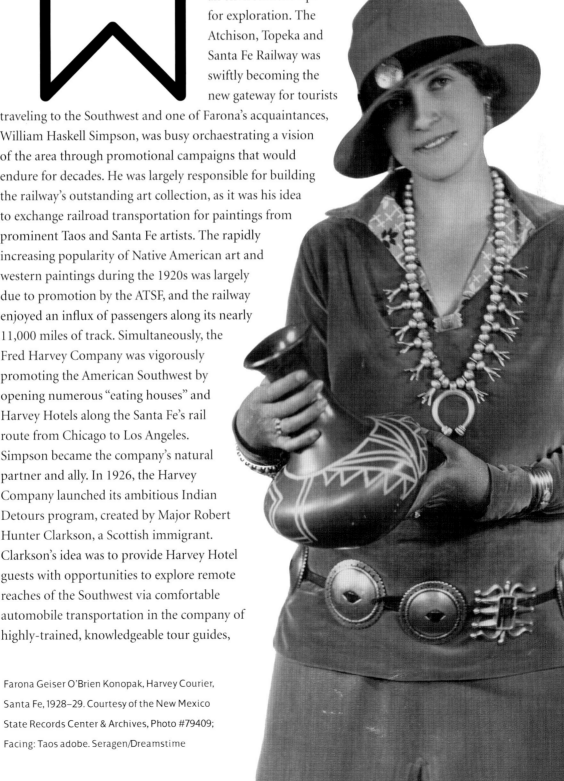

Scenes on the Indian detour

The Moving Pictures
of Farona Konopak

DOTTIE DIAMANT

When Farona Konopak arrived in New Mexico in 1918 she encountered an environment ripe for exploration. The Atchison, Topeka and Santa Fe Railway was swiftly becoming the new gateway for tourists traveling to the Southwest and one of Farona's acquaintances, William Haskell Simpson, was busy orchaestrating a vision of the area through promotional campaigns that would endure for decades. He was largely responsible for building the railway's outstanding art collection, as it was his idea to exchange railroad transportation for paintings from prominent Taos and Santa Fe artists. The rapidly increasing popularity of Native American art and western paintings during the 1920s was largely due to promotion by the ATSF, and the railway enjoyed an influx of passengers along its nearly 11,000 miles of track. Simultaneously, the Fred Harvey Company was vigorously promoting the American Southwest by opening numerous "eating houses" and Harvey Hotels along the Santa Fe's rail route from Chicago to Los Angeles. Simpson became the company's natural partner and ally. In 1926, the Harvey Company launched its ambitious Indian Detours program, created by Major Robert Hunter Clarkson, a Scottish immigrant. Clarkson's idea was to provide Harvey Hotel guests with opportunities to explore remote reaches of the Southwest via comfortable automobile transportation in the company of highly-trained, knowledgeable tour guides,

Farona Geiser O'Brien Konopak, Harvey Courier, Santa Fe, 1928–29. Courtesy of the New Mexico State Records Center & Archives, Photo #79409; Facing: Taos adobe. Seragen/Dreamstime

Scenes on the Indian detour

Above: A Harvey Girl filling a coffee cup from an urn behind train depot lunch counter at El Ortiz, Lamy, New Mexico, ca. 1900. Fred Harvey photo, courtesy NPS

Facing: The "Fred Harvey Bunch," a group of thirteen employees, including five Harvey Girls, stands by the Bright Angel Hotel, ca. 1915. Photo by T. L. Brown, courtesy NPS

all women, who were referred to as "couriers." Along the way, guests, or "detourists," stayed at the Harvey Company's elaborate and gracious hotels, many designed by the famed Santa Fe Railroad architect Mary E. J. Colter, and shopped at the hotel "curio" shops that were filled with fine examples of American Indian pottery, baskets, textiles, and jewelry. Evening entertainment at Harvey Hotel outposts in Santa Fe, Winslow, and the Grand Canyon included slideshows and lectures about the next day's excursions and upcoming attractions.

Farona Konopak met W. H. Simpson around 1927 and appealed to him for a position as a courier on the Detours program. Simpson sent a personal letter of recommendation on January 21, 1928, to Roger Birdseye, publicity and advertising manager in Santa Fe for the Detours program, requesting "any help you can give [her] in getting located." By spring 1928, Farona was working as a Harvey courier leading trips for detourists from all over the country. One wrote that she "was ever-mindful of the interests and comforts of her guests on the trip. We were so pleased with her that when we returned to Santa Fe a few weeks later we arranged a special trip from Santa Fe to Taos pueblo on condition that [she] should accompany us." During her days as a courier, Farona carefully assembled a state-of-the-art 16mm film kit housed in a custom-made wooden box that a Harvey or other car could easily accommodate. She used it to film interesting and unique scenes of people and places, some of which became Fred Harvey promotional film strips.

One such film, entitled "Scenes on the Indian Detours," likely commissioned by the Harvey Company, shows Harvey touring cars at prominent landmarks such as the Grand Canyon,

Calling card. Farona Konopak collection. Courtesy of the New Mexico State Records Center & Archives

Canyon de Chelly, Mesa Verde, and Bandelier National Monument. There are images of the Hopi villages in Arizona as well as the New Mexican pueblos, and one noteworthy image depicts the famous potter Maria Martinez outside her home with an eager detourist admiring a finished vessel. Indian ceremonial dances were also recorded (a practice now strictly forbidden, as is most photography) and various images of distinguished Harvey Hotels like El Ortiz in Lamy, the Alvarado in Albuquerque, and El Navajo in Gallup, New Mexico, which have sadly all now been demolished. La Fonda Hotel in Santa Fe, which was remodeled by Mary Colter and noted architect John Gaw Meem in the late 1920s, is repeatedly showcased through Farona's lens, as it was the headquarters for the Detours program and an attractive destination for travelers. Farona met her future husband, Lothar Konopak, a successful accountant from Ohio, on one of the Detours. After the couple married in 1929 she left the Harvey Company, and in 1935 the pair built a beautiful home in the heart of Santa Fe's artistic community on the famous El Camino del Monte Sol. Farona's marriage afforded her the leisure to be an enthusiastic explorer of the Southwest for the rest of her life—and to continue recording her experiences on film.

Farona occupied a unique place and time in history and enjoyed an intimate access to people and places that would be virtually impossible to duplicate today. Films shot in the mid-1930s by Farona and her husband highlight various Indian pueblos and the village of Taos, including what appears to be the only known moving footage of influential Taos Society of Artists painters Joseph Henry Sharp, E. I. Couse, and Bert G. Phillips. The ebullient Farona appears in several scenes encouraging friends to warm up to the camera. Some of her Indian and Hispanic acquaintances seem to hesitate before the camera, but others, like J. H. Sharp, appear very comfortable. The painter comically teases the filmmaker with his paintbrush and laughs with Farona and an unidentified friend.

These film reels—prototypical "home movies"—show a wonderful and easy familiarity between Konopak and her subjects that is wholly different in feel from the static still images of the period. The active images capture a sense of personalities and locales in the unique and immediate way that only motion pictures can. Popular 20th-century western movies like the big-screen epics of John Ford showed the American Southwest as a scenic backdrop against which great societal themes such as "good vs. evil," "manifest destiny," and the "march of civilization" played out. These elaborate, highly-staged productions helped shape America's sense of identity and are indeed an important part of our film history. Farona's small-scale films, so touchingly human, show us a closeup view. In popular movies, stars such as John Wayne acted out the rough and tumble cowboy or lawman in a vast, remote, and often dangerous West full of "hostile" Indians, but Farona actually experienced the "Golden Age" of the Southwest—making herself into a passionate advocate for and chronicler of its natural and cultural heritage. Farona's "homemade" films show the Southwestern landscape and people as they truly were, on a deeply intimate and personal scale. These images are a magical portal to a long-lost time made visible today through the eye of this dedicated and passionate observer.

DOTTIE DIAMANT, a partner in Fine Arts of the Southwest, Inc., Santa Fe, New Mexico, is currently researching the life and times of Farona Konopak for a future endeavor.

The Farona Konopak materials are in the collection of Rennard Strickland. Images shown are of Farona Konopak's film kit and stills from travel reels she produced.

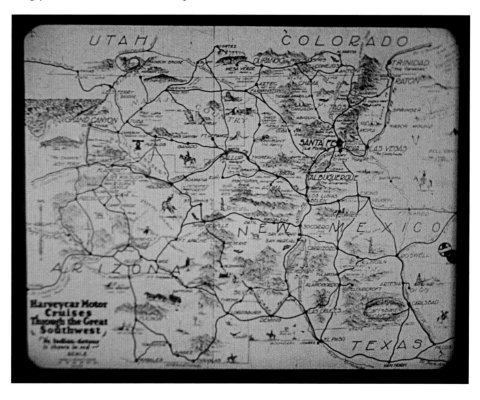

Approximately 65 minutes of Farona's films have been transferred to video. To watch them as YouTubes, type these addresses into your browser or take a shortcut and point your smartphone at the QRs below.

http://www.youtube.com/watch?v=F6cHXW2iaLg&feature=plcp
http://www.youtube.com/watch?v=wudnqVi9qqY&feature=relmfu
http://www.youtube.com/watch?v=0QijmP8qjns&feature=relmfu
http://www.youtube.com/watch?v=C6MulKSmQRk&feature=relmfu
http://www.youtube.com/watch?v=uNydeIPw0aQ&feature=relmfu

Millions of years of patient erosion have nibbled at the southwestern
edges of the Colorado Plateau, exposing its colorful core around
Sedona, Arizona. Photo by Ted Grussing

technicolor rocks

JOE MCNEILL

Monument Valley has the cachet of its association with John Ford. Lone Pine in California has the numbers—over 400 films have been made there. But Sedona, Arizona, is American film in microcosm, from silent movies to early talkies to B Westerns to World War II propaganda to film noir to 3-D movies to rock 'n' roll to 1970s road pictures—a visual record of 20th-century popular culture. Although Sedona played host to more than sixty film productions between 1923 and 1973, it was never really known to the world at large as a filming location, even in its prime. Studio public relations departments during the Golden Age of Hollywood rarely mentioned it by name, and on the rare occasion when they did, it was usually incorrectly.

The movie filmed in Sedona that gets my vote for the one everyone should see is *Broken Arrow* (1950). Most people today probably aren't aware of how important the film was to its time, and how unique it was that the good guys happened to be Indians. *Broken Arrow* is historically significant for another reason, too. It was one of the first films written in secret by a member of the "Hollywood Ten," the group that was blacklisted in the late 1940s and sent to jail because of their refusal to admit to membership in the Communist Party.

Much is surprising in Sedona's film history, but perhaps most shocking to many would be the existence of a film called *Der Kaiser von Kalifornien* (1936). Joseph Goebbels, Hitler's minister of propaganda, used modern technologies of the 1930s, including motion pictures, to promote the Nazi agenda. One of the cornerstones of Nazi doctrine was the need for *Lebensraum*—"living space" for the German people—which was the major motivation behind Hitler's territorial aggression. *Lebensraum* is at the root of *Der Kaiser*'s plot, and Sedona is specifically shown in the film as the Promised Land. Exterior scenes were also shot at the Grand Canyon and Death Valley.

I was also surprised by what we learned about filming locations for *Stagecoach*. The old *Coconino Sun*, a weekly paper published in Flagstaff, is a good resource for researching movie history of the area. It took years, but we searched through every single issue from 1923 into the early 1950s. Along the way we stumbled upon reports that some filming for *Stagecoach* took place in Sedona. In three separate reports published in the *Coconino Sun,* before, during, and after shooting, *Stagecoach* locations in Arizona were specified as Monument Valley, Cameron, Oak Creek Canyon, Schnebly Hill [on the Mogollon Rim], and areas near Phoenix. The accepted backstory about the making of *Stagecoach* is that Harry Goulding of Goulding's Lodge drove to Hollywood with snapshots of Monument Valley and talked John Ford into going there to shoot. According to the first *Sun* report, however, about a month before shooting began, the film company contacted Lee Doyle, Sedona's local movie coordinator, who drove the director around northern Arizona for a few days to scout locations—standard operating procedure for a film company planning to shoot in the area. I was able to later confirm this by locating a copy of the telegram sent to Doyle to alert him of Ford's imminent arrival in Flagstaff. Film history continues in the making, and its backstories can be as rich as onscreen drama.

Excerpted from *Arizona's Little Hollywood: Sedona and Northern Arizona's Forgotten Film History 1923–1973,* by Joe McNeill (Northedge, 2010). Contact info@arizonaslittlehollywood.com.

MAKING MOVIES AROUND THE COLORADO PLATEAU REGION

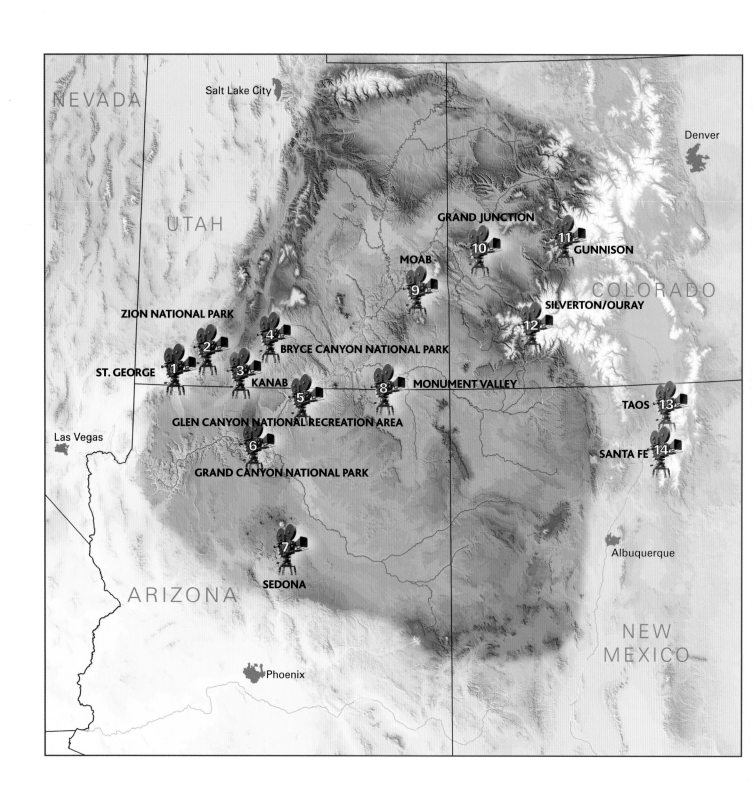

NEVADA

Salt Lake City

UTAH

Denver

GRAND JUNCTION

10

11 GUNNISON

MOAB

9

COLORADO

ZION NATIONAL PARK

SILVERTON/OURAY

4

12

2

BRYCE CANYON NATIONAL PARK

ST. GEORGE

1

3 KANAB

MONUMENT VALLEY

TAOS 13

5

8

Las Vegas

GLEN CANYON NATIONAL RECREATION AREA

SANTA FE 14

6

GRAND CANYON NATIONAL PARK

Albuquerque

7

ARIZONA

SEDONA

NEW
MEXICO

Phoenix

HOT SPOTS FOR FILMING ON THE COLORADO PLATEAU

A GEOGRAPHICAL FILMOGRAPHY

A SELECTION OF MOVIES FILMED ON THE COLORADO PLATEAU

1914	The Bargain
1915	The Great Divide
1923	The Call of the Canyon
1924	Deadwood Coach
1925	The Vanishing American
1926	Forlorn River
1927	Nevada
1928	The Vanishing Pioneer
1928	Kit Carson
1929	In Old Arizona
1931	Cimarron
1932	Robbers' Roost
1935	Der Kaiser von Kalifornien
1937	Black Stallion
1938	Out West with the Hardys
1938	The Cowboy and the Lady
1939	Union Pacific
1939	Stagecoach
1940	Billy the Kid
1940	The Westerner
1040	The Grapes of Wrath
1943	My Friend Flicka
1944	Tall in the Saddle
1946	Angel and the Badman
1946	The Harvey Girls
1946	My Darling Clementine
1947	The Strawberry Roan
1948	The Treasure of the Sierra Madre
1949	Fort Apache
1949	Copper Canyon
1949	She Wore a Yellow Ribbon
1949	Wagon Master
1950	Rio Grande
1950	The Battle at Apache Pass
1950	Broken Arrow
1951	The Half-Breed
1952	High Noon
1952	Viva Zapata!
1953	Johnny Guitar
1953	Taza, Son of Cochise
1954	Broken Lance

1954	Smoke Signal
1956	The Last Wagon
1956	3:10 to Yuma
1956	The Searchers
1958	Warlock
1959	Ten Who Dared
1960	Sergeant Rutledge
1961	The Comancheros
1963	The Greatest Story Ever Told
1963	Cheyenne Autumn
1964	Rio Conchos
1964	The Rounders
1966	Wild Rovers
1966	Fade In
1967	Brighty of Grand Canyon
1967	Blue
1967	Stay Away, Joe
1968	Planet of the Apes
1968	2001: A Space Odyssey
1969	Easy Rider
1969	Butch Cassidy and the Sundance Kid
1972	Alias Smith and Jones
1973	Harry and Tonto
1975	Against a Crooked Sky
1979	The Electric Horseman
1982	Spacehunter
1984	Choke Canyon
1985	MacGyver
1987	Nightmare at Noon
1988	Sundown: Vampires in Retreat
1988	Indiana Jones and the Last Crusade
1990	Thelma and Louise
1990	Back to the Future
1992	Knights
1992	Slaughter of the Innocents
1993	Geronimo: An American Legend
1993	City Slickers II
1993	Lightning Jack
1994	The Great American West
1995	Larger Than Life
1995	Riders of the Purple Sage

1995	Broken Arrow
1996	Breakdown
1996	Con-Air
1997	Lost Treasure of Dos Santos
1998	Chill Factor
1998	Galaxy Quest
1999	The Adventures of Joe Dirt
1999	Mission Impossible II
1999	Vertical Limit
2000	Nurse Betty
2001	Touched by an Angel
2002	Austin Powers 3
2002	Goldmember
2005	Don't Come Knocking
2007	The Canyon
2008	Star Trek
2009	Remember I'll Always Love You
2009	Crazy Heart
2010	127 Hours
2010	John Carter of Mars
2010	Guns, Girls, and Gambling
2012	After Earth
2012	The Lone Ranger

. . . and next time you're watching a movie with great scenery and wondering where it was made, check it out at http://www.nps.gov/pub_aff/movie.htm or point your phone at the QR below to see a list of films made on public lands. Since 1910, filmmakers have been coming to national parks year after year to capture majestic scenery for their productions.

Moab's Movie Museum

SAM WAINER

A life-size cardboard statue of John Wayne; the dummy of Thelma (Geena Davis) that went over the canyon edge in the closing scene of *Thelma and Louise*; the original script from *The Battle of Apache Pass.* These are just a few of the movie items that can be found at the Moab Museum of Film and Western Heritage located in the Red Cliffs Lodge near Moab, Utah. One might wonder how this movie memorabilia ended up in such a remote location.

The answer is . . . the property the lodge occupies was a prime location for filming Westerns in the 1950s and 60s. Colin Fryer, owner of Red Cliffs Ranch and proprietor of the Red Cliff Lodge, bought the ranch from the White family in 1990. Along with a nice herd of cattle and beautiful acreage on the Colorado River, Fryer inherited the rich film history associated with the landscape.

George and Essie White were married in 1929 and shortly took over operations of the White Ranch, located near Moab. The ranch sits on the banks of the Colorado River in a remote setting known as Professor Valley. George and Essie knew the unique landscape that was linked to their everyday lives was special and they longed for a way to share this amazing place with the rest of the world. That opportunity came in 1949, when director John Ford was looking for an alternative movie location to Monument Valley, having just completed his fourth film there.

When Ford arrived in Moab, he was introduced to George White, who promptly took him to Nine Mile Bottom on the Colorado River just north of his ranch. Looking downriver past the spires of Fisher Towers with the La Sal Mountains looming large in the background, Ford exclaimed, "That's the greatest sight I've ever seen." The director decided on the spot to shoot his next picture, *Rio Grande,* at the location.

George saw the economic potential the film industry held for the Moab area. He also saw the need for coordinating the many demands a large movie production could place on a small community. In 1949, he founded the Moab Movie Committee to promote the area's unique scenery to the film industry and to act as a liaison between the movie studios and the town of Moab. Because of George White's foresight, today the Moab to Monument Valley Film Commission is the longest-running film commission in North America.

After the completion of *Rio Grande,* between 1950 and 1964, *Ten Who Dared, The Commancheros, Cheyenne Autumn, Battle of Apache Pass, Taza Son of Cochise* and *Rio Conchos* were all filmed on the ranch and surrounding lands. John Wayne, Maureen O'Hara, Ben Johnson, Rock Hudson, Henry Fonda, Anthony Quinn, Lee Marvin, Richard Widmark, James Stewart, and Richard Boone have all worked on location at what is now the Red Cliffs Ranch.

As the number of locally filmed movies and television commercials grew, so did the idea of establishing a Moab film history museum. The Moab Film Commission took on the project, and in 1985, as director of the commission, Bette Stanton began collecting local film memorabilia. Her goal was to develop a movie museum, which she eventually established in the Moab Film Commission office.

Colin Fryer purchased the White Family Ranch in 1990 and began construction of Red Cliffs Lodge on the property in 1998. Colin realized how much of the film commission's movie memorabilia had come from his recently acquired property, and thought it would be a good idea to bring the history back to the place it was created. Bette Stanton's original collection, along with other movie memorabilia, is now housed at the Moab Museum of Film and Western Heritage at the Red Cliffs Lodge.

The museum is free to the public and open daily. It offers a glimpse into the heyday of western filmmaking. On display are production photographs, movie posters, autographed scripts, and props. One of the more unique items is a group of models of the sets from *Riders of the Purple Sage.* These were built before the sets were constructed to get a sense of how everything would look. A portion of the museum is dedicated to displays about the western ranching heritage of Professor Valley. There are also tributes to directors and information about the many fashion shoots, print ads, and TV commercials shot in the area.

Whether you're a movie buff or just interested in western history, a visit to the Moab Museum of Film and Western Heritage is entertaining and informative. Red Cliffs Lodge is located at mile post 14 on Highway 128 in Moab, Utah.

For a virtual tour of the museum, visit http://www.redcliffslodge.com /images/virtual-tours/museum/

〰〰〰 Fifty Filmed in Moab 〰〰〰

1939 – Stagecoach
1949 - Wagon Master
1950 - Rio Grande
1950 - The Battle At Apache Pass
1953 - Taza, son of Cochise
1958 – Warlock
1959 - Ten Who Dared
1961 – Comancheros
1963 - The Greatest Story Ever Told
1963 - Cheyenne Autumn
1964 - Rio Conchos
1966 - Wild Rovers
1966 - Fade In
1967 - Blue
1975 - Against a Crooked Sky
1982 - Spacehunter
1984 - Choke Canyon

1985 – MacGyver
1987 - Nightmare at Noon
1988 - Sundown: Vampires in Retreat
1988 - Indiana Jones and the Last Crusade
1990 - Thelma and Louise
1992 – Knights
1992 - Slaughter of the Innocents
1993 - Geronimo: An American Legend
1993 - City Slickers II
1993 - Lightning Jack
1994 - The Great American West
1995 - Larger Than Life
1995 - Riders of the Purple Sage
1996 – Breakdown
1996 - Con-Air
1997 - Lost Treasure of Dos Santos
1998 - Chill Factor

1998 - Galaxy Quest
1999 - The Adventures of Joe Dirt
1999 - Mission Impossible II
1999 - Vertical Limit
2000 - Nurse Betty
2001 - Touched by an Angel
2002 - Austin Powers 3
2005 - Don't Come Knocking
2007 - The Canyon
2008 - Star Trek
2009 - Remember I'll Always Love You
2010 - 127 Hours
2010 - John Carter of Mars
2010 - Guns, Girls, and Gambling
2012 - After Earth
2012 - The Lone Ranger

meep meep!

ICON: *Broadly, an image, sign, or likeness that stands for a concept either concretely or by analogy; particularly in modern culture, a face, picture, edifice, landscape, or other entity that is readily recognized as representing or embodying certain qualities. For example, Marilyn Monroe is an icon of Hollywood sensuality. Monument Valley is an icon of the West.*

The desert Southwest is home to many icons: iconic experiences like summertime family road trips, iconic images like fencelines dotted with tumbleweed and endless ribbons of road that say expanse and adventure. Creatures too, including cartoonist Chuck Jones's tuft-headed, faster-than-the-eye-can-follow roadrunner, the hapless but unstoppable Wile E. Coyote—and, recently joining them, a personable, urbane gecko.

In brief commercial spots on television, the now-familiar Geico gecko is wandering America from New York to Chicago to Monument Valley. There, he finds himself in the same striking landscape that awaits any who journey to the Southwest, whether in cartoons, western movies, or real travels. But some strange things are happening. Anvils and pianos fall from the sky. A roadrunner comes roaring across the landscape to stop, hop, and *meep-meep!* before he zooms away in a trail of dust. Just on his heels comes a determined cartoon coyote—the very icon of fanatic dedication to the chase, the unswerving beta-tester, the apparent holder of a limitless credit line at ACME products. He stops to view the gecko. An image of gecko dinner floats above him in cartoon space. But before he can lunge, a huge ACME safe falls from the sky. Boom! Poof!

The gecko wanders off remarking about the beautiful landscape, so full of of strange and inexplicable experiences. It's a TV moment as layered as the landscape—iconic place, check. Childhood memory of movie cartoons in darkened theaters (for Baby Boomers, for sure), check. Recognizable animated creatures, ditto, check. The Warner Brothers/ Merrie Melodies creation meets a car insurance company's charming icon (voiced by English comedian and actor Jake Wood for the Martin Agency, creator of the Geico ads). The space of imagination and humor meets the space of western terrain. And much is set in motion, on screen and in the mind. —Julie Reichert and Carol Haralson

Coyote and Roadrunner, which first appeared in Looney Tunes and Merrie Melodies cartoons in 1948, were the creations of animator Chuck Jones (1912–2002). To view an Archive of American Television interview with Jones, visit http://www.emmytvlegends.org/interviews/people/chuck-jones